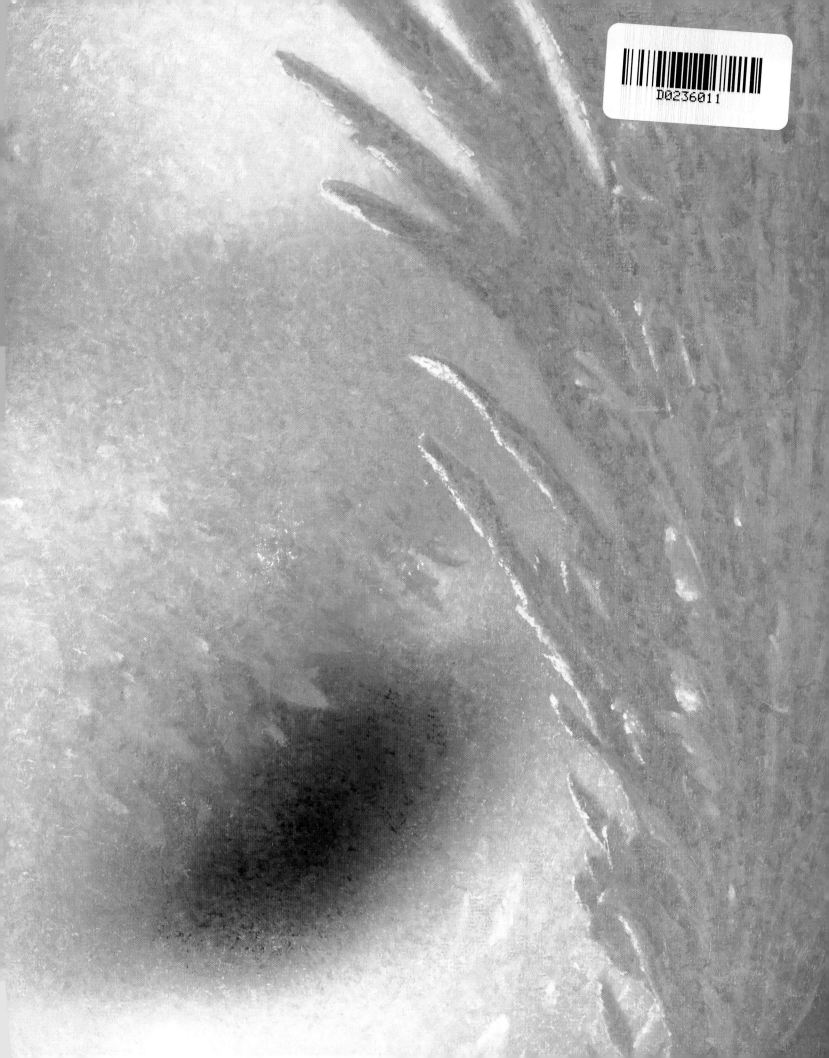

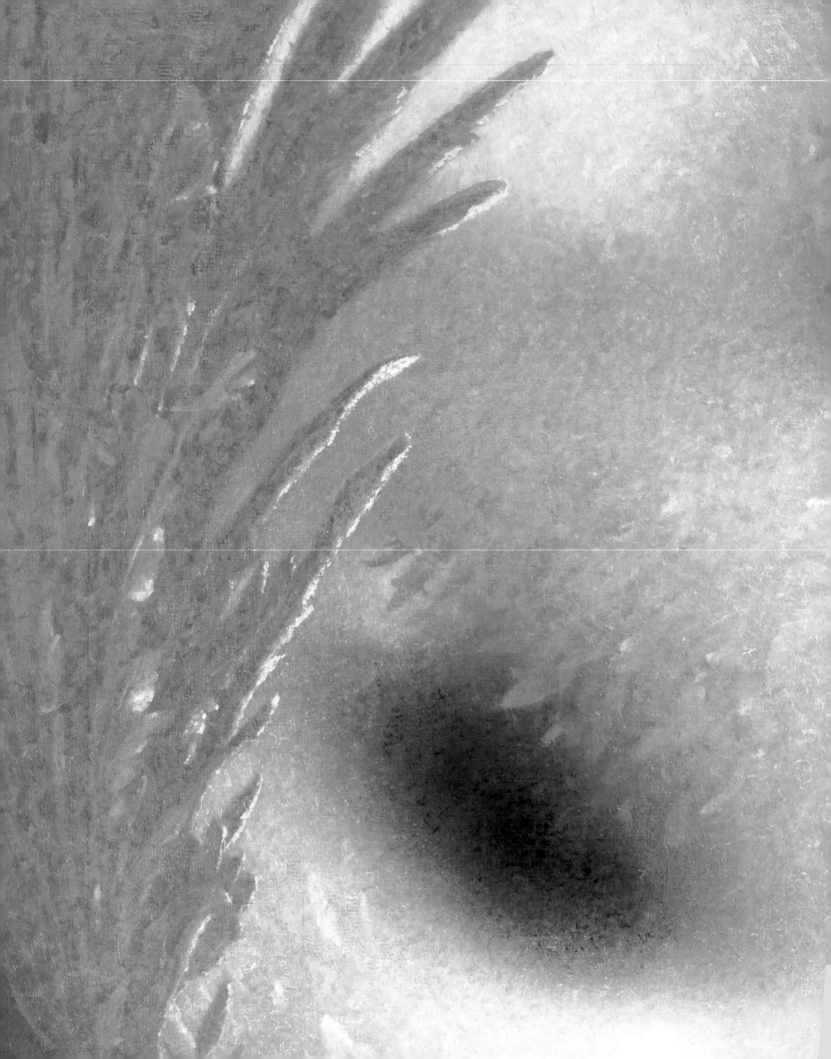

This is the star

This is the star

Joyce Dunbar
illustrated by Gary Blythe

★

DOUBLEDAY
London · New York · Toronto · Sydney · Auckland

This is the star in the sky.

These are the shepherds watching by night
That saw the star in the sky.

This is the angel shining bright,
Who came to the shepherds watching by night
That saw the star in the sky.

This is the donkey with precious load
Trudging the long and weary road,
Looked on by the angel shining bright,
Who came to the shepherds watching by night
That saw the star in the sky.

This is the inn where the only room
Was a stable out in the lamplit gloom
For the donkey and his precious load
Who trudged the long and weary road,
Looked on by the angel shining bright,
Who came to the shepherds watching by night
That saw the star in the sky.

This is the ox and this is the ass
Who saw such wonders come to pass
At the darkened inn where the only room
Was a stable out in the lamplit gloom
For the donkey and his precious load
Who trudged the long and weary road,
Looked on by the angel shining bright,
Who came to the shepherds watching by night
That saw the star in the sky.

This is the manger, warm with hay
Wherein a new-born baby lay.
This is the ox and this the ass
Who saw these wonders come to pass
At the darkened inn where the only room
Was a stable out in the lamplit gloom
For the donkey and his precious load
Who trudged the long and weary road,
Looked on by the angel shining bright,
Who came to the shepherds watching by night
That saw the star in the sky.

This is the gold, and fragrant myrrh

And frankincense, the gifts that were

Placed by the manger warm with hay

Wherein a new-born baby lay.

This is the ox and this the ass

Who saw these wonders come to pass

At the darkened inn where the only room

Was a stable out in the lamplit gloom

For the donkey and his precious load

Who trudged the long and weary road,

Looked on by the angel shining bright,

Who came to the shepherds watching by night

That saw the star in the sky.

These are the wise men come from afar
Who also saw and followed the star,
Bearing the gold, and fragrant myrrh
And frankincense, the gifts that were
Placed by the manger warm with hay
Wherein a new-born baby lay.
This is the ox and this the ass
Who saw these wonders come to pass
At the darkened inn where the only room
Was a stable out in the lamplit gloom
For the donkey and his precious load
Who trudged the long and weary road,
Looked on by the angel shining bright,
Who came to the shepherds watching by night
That saw the star in the sky.

This is the child that was born.

This is the Christ child born to be king
While hosts of heavenly angels sing.
These are the wise men come from afar
Who also saw and followed the star,
Bearing the gold, and fragrant myrrh
And frankincense, the gifts that were
Placed by the manger warm with hay
Wherein a new-born baby lay.
This is the ox and this the ass
Who saw these wonders come to pass
At the darkened inn where the only room
Was a stable out in the lamplit gloom
For the donkey and his precious load
Who trudged the long and weary road,
Looked on by the angel shining bright,
Who came to the shepherds watching by night
That saw the star in the sky.

Still shines the star in the sky.

Transworld Publishers Ltd
61-63 Uxbridge Road, London W5 5SA

Transworld Publishers (Australia) Pty Ltd
15-25 Helles Avenue, Moorebank, NSW 2170

Transworld Publishers (NZ) Ltd
3 William Pickering Drive, Albany, Auckland

Doubleday Canada Ltd
105 Bond Street, Toronto, Ontario M5B 1Y3

Published in 1996 by Doubleday
a division of Transworld Publishers Ltd

Text copyright © 1996 by Joyce Dunbar
Illustrations copyright © 1996 Gary Blythe
Designed by Ian Butterworth

A catalogue record for this book is available from the British Library

ISBN 0 385 406029

Printed in Belgium by Proost

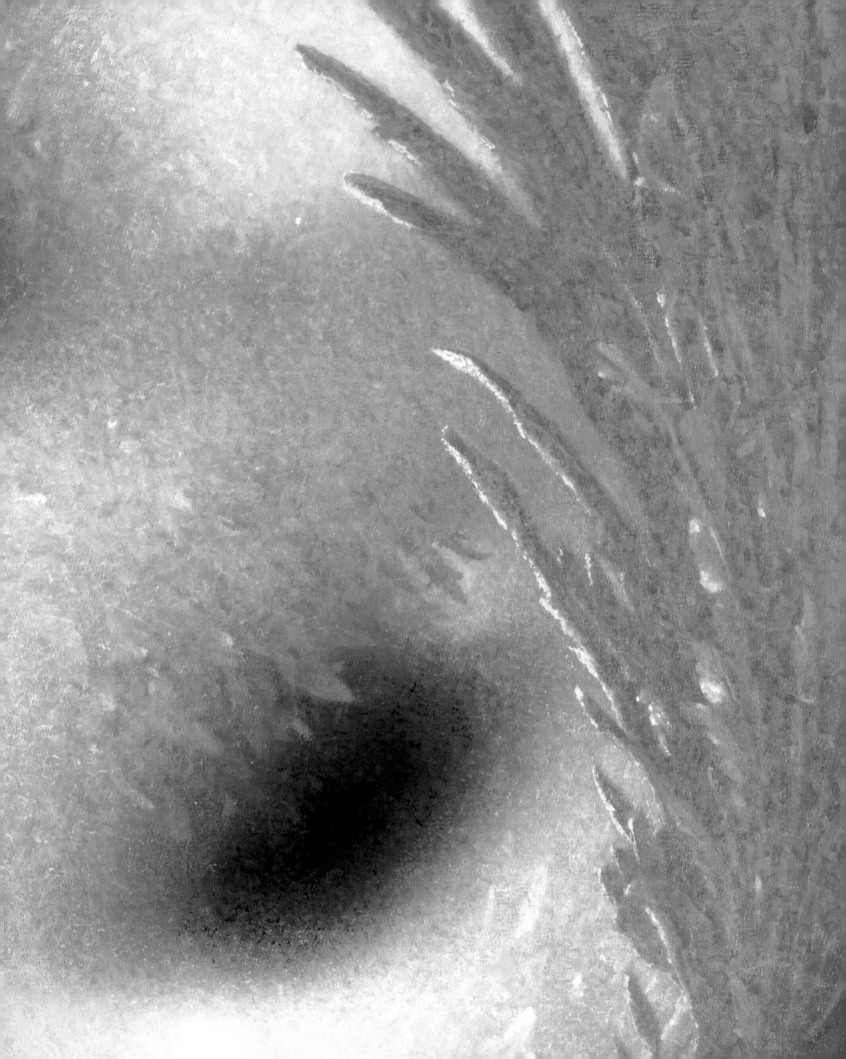

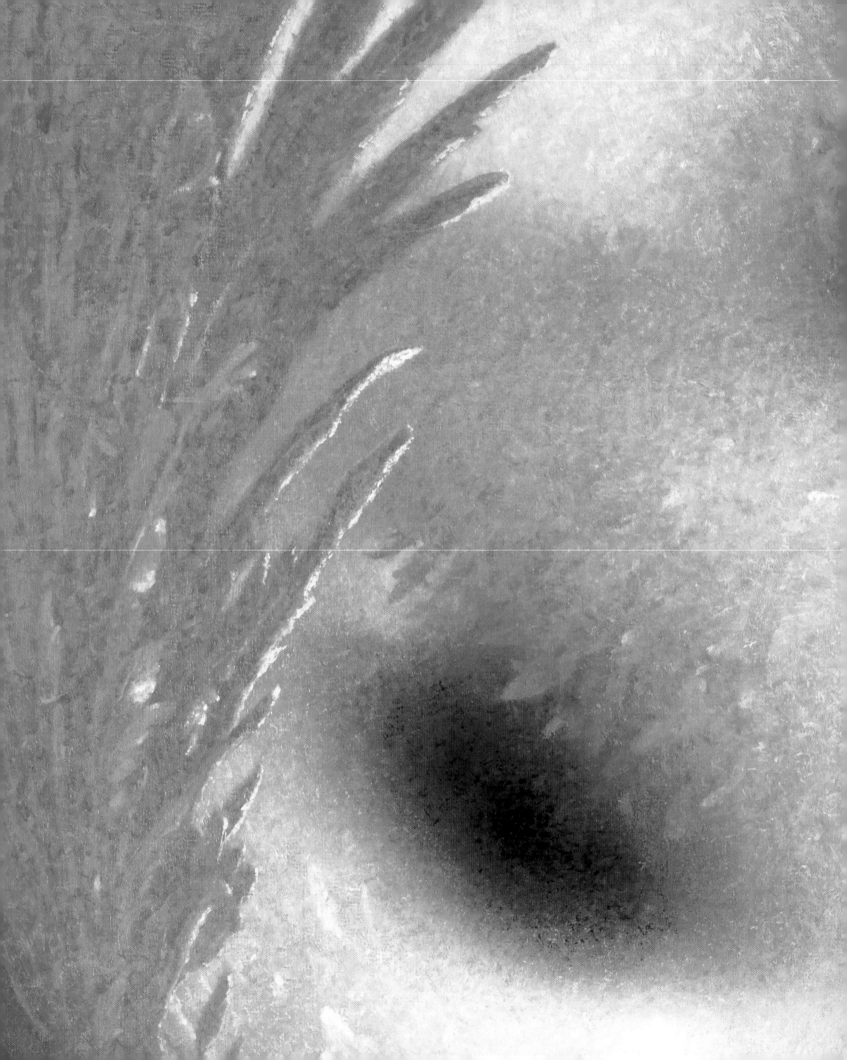